The I

a very tall tale

TREVOR
PYE

Chapter 1

I remember the day I was picked to run in The Big Race. It felt like the worst day of my life. The worst day in the history of the universe! I felt very sorry for myself.

The race was for all the schools in our area. But my school, Duck Lake Primary School, was very small. There were only eleven students – and we weren't very good at sport.

Our head teacher, Mr Springler, picked me because I was tall. I had the longest legs in the school.

Duck Lake Primary School had never won The Big Race. Every year when the poster was put up, we all got the shivers. Nobody wanted to be Duck Lake's runner.

But every year, Mr Springler picked someone to run in the race. "If you're not in, you can't win" was one of his favourite sayings.

And this year, the prize was extra special!

I felt terrible. Our school was the worst in the history of the world at running. Everyone would be looking at me. But there was no way out! I even tried begging with Mr Springler, but it was no use.

I would have to run with the whizz-kids from the other schools. They were all faster than me. I could remember them well. Ben Banks, last year's winner. Milly McMinn, as strong as an ox. Dan Walker, with legs like an antelope ...

It was too terrible to think about!

Chapter 2

There was only a week to go until the race, and my body looked like a beanpole. I had to do some exercise.

The kids at school tried to cheer me up ...

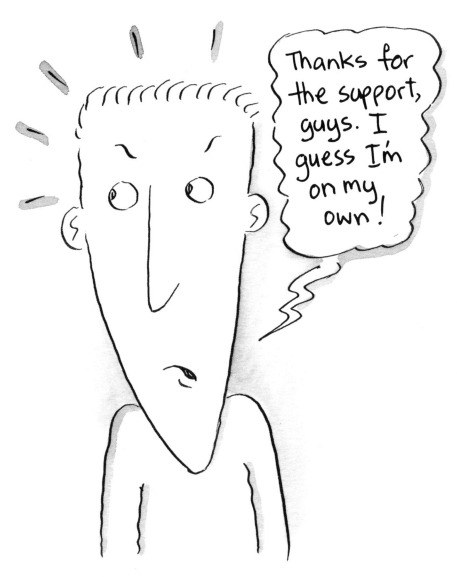

... but that didn't work.
So I did some more exercise.

I did more press-ups.

I skipped.

I did one-armed chin-ups.

And I ate a lot of Dad's special cereal.

At last, on the day before the race, I knew I was as fit as I could be. The problem was, I was *so* tired from all that exercise!

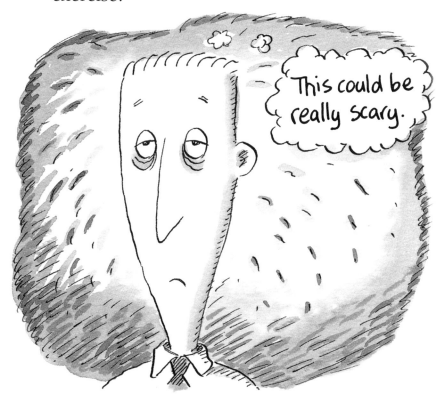

That night, I had to go to a "get-together" to meet the other runners.

And it *was* scary! There was Ben Banks and Milly McMinn and Dan Walker – and some other kids I didn't know.

When I got home, I couldn't get to sleep. I was scared I'd dream about the race.

Next morning, I walked to school very slowly. Even my friend Richie couldn't cheer me up.

"Hey, Trevor. Cheer up. Do you want to hear a good joke?"

"Not really, Richie."

Mr Springler was waiting at the school gates. He looked really happy. He really thought that I could win! That made me feel even worse.

Chapter 3

We all got into the school van. Mr Springler drove to the sports field at the edge of town. That's where the race was going to start. I just stared out of the window. I had butterflies in my stomach, but the other kids were having a great time.

When we got to the field, Mr Springler took me to a big tent.

I was weighed ...

and measured ...

and they gave me a life jacket.

What's this for?

Then they gave me the most important thing – the map of the race.

Suddenly a loud voice came over the loudspeaker. "All runners to the starting line, please." The Big Race was about to begin! I looked at the other nine runners. They all looked *super* fit.

The starter held up the gun and called –

Ten pairs of legs sprang into action.
Well, nine pairs, really. Mine hopped
into action.

We raced off the sports field and down a track. The track led to Wild Rapid River. So far, I was keeping up with the others. Maybe all my exercise had worked.

But Wild Rapid River was very fast. Eight runners made it across. Then Dave Dickens slipped. I grabbed his arm, but we both floated away – along the river and over a waterfall. Thank goodness for the life jackets.

I swam to the shore at the bottom of the cliff. Dave Dickens was not so lucky. He floated out to sea. Luckily, a passing tanker picked him up.

When I got my breath back, I ran up the beach and saw the other runners. They were climbing down the cliffs.

Suddenly, a huge wave from the tanker crashed onto the beach. We were all knocked flat.

It was a terrible and frightening sight.

We were soaked to the skin, but nobody was hurt. Everyone jumped up and ran to the cliff. It looked *very* steep!

Up the cliff we went, and I was still with the others! When I got to the top, I checked my map. Then off I raced to the Bald Eagle Mountains.

When I got to the Bald Eagle Mountains, the other runners had left me behind. I was puffed out, and my legs were sore.

As I ran into the mountains, I looked up. I could see big, black clouds, and large drops of rain started to fall. Everything was getting darker *and* scarier.

Chapter 4

As I ran along the track, the rain got worse and worse. I think that was when the map fell out of my pocket.

Soon I came to a fork in the track, but the sign had been washed out by the rain. I felt for my map – it was gone!

There was only one thing left to do. I reached into my pocket and pulled out a coin.

It was tails, so I took the right path. But it was the *wrong* path. Before long, I was lost – and still the rain poured down. I was just about to give up when I saw some shelter. It was a cave.

I sat there in the cave. It was dark and creepy, but it was out of the rain. As I sat watching the storm, I felt a cool breeze on my neck.

I ran through the cold, dark cave. It wasn't long before I saw light.

I walked out onto a rocky ledge. The sky was clear and bright. The storm had gone, but I didn't know where I was.

Suddenly, something swooped down on me. It was a very rare, giant bald eagle. It picked me up in its huge claws and flew off into the sky.

The other runners were having problems as well. One of them had been picked up by a giant bald eagle too. It carried him to its nest, high in the mountains.

Milly McMinn and Ben Banks got as far as the Badlands Forest. Then they were chased up a tree by Badlands Forest wolves!

The others had all made it through the Bald Eagle Mountains and the Badlands Forest. They were just going to cross Wild Rapid River for the last time.

I was not so lucky. When I opened my eyes and looked down, I could see the ground – way below.

I screamed and fainted. I must have given the eagle a shock because it dropped me.

Luckily, I landed in some thick, soft bushes. I got up and wobbled towards the finishing line. But Dan Walker was right behind me. He ran like the wind.

Mr Springler and the kids from Duck Lake cheered. They couldn't believe their eyes. Just as Dan was going to pass me, I tripped and fell ...

... over the finishing line.

I beat Dan by a nose! Mr Springler and the kids went wild. For the first time ever, Duck Lake Primary School had won The Big Race.

I didn't know I had won the race. I was lying across the finishing line, exhausted and fast asleep.

That's how I remember the day I won The Big Race. I'm *sure* that's just how it happened.